INTRODUCTION

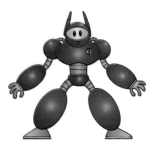

Welcome to **How To Draw People.** We all know that pictures can look really intimidating to attempt. They can seem complicated or difficult, and it is sometimes hard to even know where to start. The great thing about this book, though, is that it breaks down even the most detailed pictures into easily understandable steps, so you can start drawing almost right away.

We all know that drawing is a creative pastime, but people don't always realize that it's technical too. Don't let that put you off though. What it means is that pictures are constructed from various geometrical shapes, and it's possible, with practice, to train yourself to spot these shapes easily. For example, a person's head is shaped very much like an upside-down egg. This and many other secrets are all revealed in this book, so you'll become an expert in no time at all.

MATERIALS

The most important materials you'll need for getting started are a pencil and some drawing paper. Pencils are graded from soft to hard. Hard pencils, such as a No. 3, produce a fine line that's good for technical drawings. Softer pencils, such as a No. 1, produce a much darker line that is ideal for artistic shading. A good general-purpose pencil to use is a standard No. 2. This will produce a solid line that is still easy to erase if you should happen to make a mistake.

Paper, like pencils, comes in many variations. There are so many different thicknesses, grades, and surface textures. For example, paper with a heavy grain is great for watercolor painting, but not so good for pen drawings. The best paper to use for reproducing the drawings in this book is plain photocopier paper. As well as being inexpensive to buy, it has a smooth surface, making it easier to erase pencil markings.

Obviously, you're going to need an eraser and a pencil sharpener too. Pencils need to be sharpened regularly so that they give an accurate and constant line. A ruler is also required for certain drawings, especially those that require making measurements, as is a black fine-line pen. Fine-line pens come in different thicknesses, and they help produce a strong outline to your work.

Other drawing tools you may want to consider are shape stencils. With some of the drawings in this book, it is easier, not to mention quicker, to use a circle and ellipse stencil. Stencils come in many other shapes, too. You can all these items from office supply outlets and hobby and craft stores.

Finally, you're going to need to use color for your pictures. Colored pencils are excellent, and you can be really accurate with them. You may prefer using watercolor paints or pastels. At the end of the day, it's up to you—it's all about whatever you feel most comfortable doing!

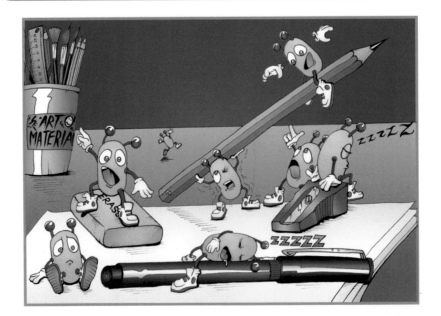

People come in all shapes and sizes, and our body shapes are constantly changing as we grow from a baby to an adult. In this chapter, we're going to look at how to draw people of different ages, and we'll also find out how to draw different facial expressions, hand shapes, and items of clothing.

In the first example, we'll be attempting to draw a young boy. The younger we are, the larger our head is in comparison with the rest of our body. This boy is roughly "five heads" tall. He has a huge grin on his face, and has clenched fists. He's wearing baggy jeans and a hooded sweatshirt.

Next we have a teenage girl. At this age, she is about "seven heads" in height. She has an expression of boredom, and her hands are flat by her sides. The clothes she's wearing is tight-fitting sports gear.

In the final example, you'll be drawing a fully-grown man. He is "eight heads" tall and has an angry expression on his face. One of his hands is open, and the other hand is slightly clenched in frustration. His tee shirt is tight-fitting, while his combat pants are baggy.

This chapter will give you a very clear idea of how to draw figures and clothing, and this is important to making many of the following chapters easier to figure out!

STEP 1

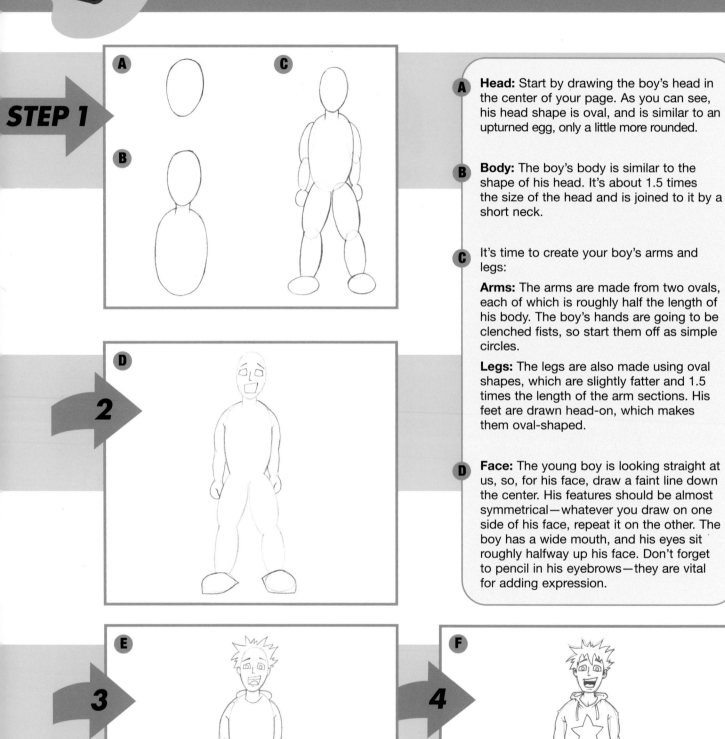

2

3

4

A **Head:** Start by drawing the boy's head in the center of your page. As you can see, his head shape is oval, and is similar to an upturned egg, only a little more rounded.

B **Body:** The boy's body is similar to the shape of his head. It's about 1.5 times the size of the head and is joined to it by a short neck.

C It's time to create your boy's arms and legs:

Arms: The arms are made from two ovals, each of which is roughly half the length of his body. The boy's hands are going to be clenched fists, so start them off as simple circles.

Legs: The legs are also made using oval shapes, which are slightly fatter and 1.5 times the length of the arm sections. His feet are drawn head-on, which makes them oval-shaped.

D **Face:** The young boy is looking straight at us, so, for his face, draw a faint line down the center. His features should be almost symmetrical—whatever you draw on one side of his face, repeat it on the other. The boy has a wide mouth, and his eyes sit roughly halfway up his face. Don't forget to pencil in his eyebrows—they are vital for adding expression.

5

6

Arms: To get the overall shape of the boy's arms, join the two ovals with a flowing outline. Next, his hands are given definition by drawing a line where his thumb is tucked into his palm.

Feet: Give the feet a rounded toe each, with a flat base. You can also draw the line where his jeans meet his shoes.

E Face: Start putting some more detail on his face: the pupils in his eyes, the tongue and teeth, some spiked hair, and his ears.

Hands: Show where the skin at the base of the boy's thumb is creased slightly—this is important because he is clenching his fists.

Clothes: This boy is wearing a baggy, hooded sweatshirt and loose, ripped jeans. His hooded top billows out at the bottom because of its elastic waistband. The sleeves do the same. The jeans, however, hang off his waist and drape over his legs.

F Clothes: The boy's sweater has a large star emblem on it. He has creased and ripped pants with turn-ups. Give his shoes some detail, such as shoelaces and rubber soles.

Hands: Add depth to the boy's hands by showing where his other fingers are bent. Remember that they are obscured slightly because of the position of his hands.

G Draw over the picture of your boy using a thin black pen. Pen in the lines you want to keep, and then erase any leftover pencil lines. Now that he's ready to color, you can start thinking about what tones you want to use.

H This boy's jeans are blue. His top is bright red, because red is a vibrant, in-your-face color, and this boy has a confident look about him. Remember that color is a great way to enhance the character of your drawings, so try to choose colors that say something about the people you are drawing.

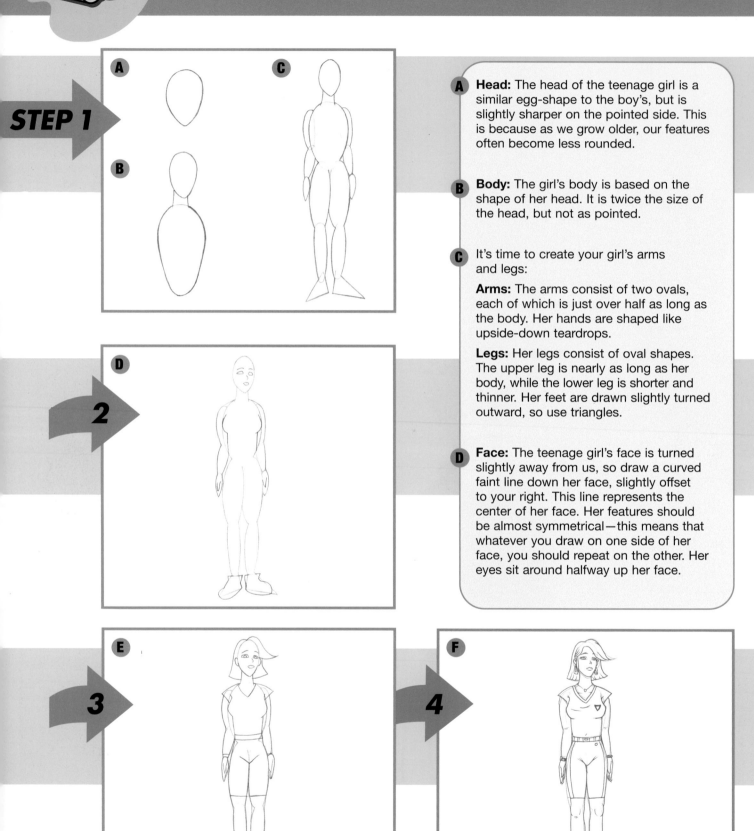

A **Head:** The head of the teenage girl is a similar egg-shape to the boy's, but is slightly sharper on the pointed side. This is because as we grow older, our features often become less rounded.

B **Body:** The girl's body is based on the shape of her head. It is twice the size of the head, but not as pointed.

C It's time to create your girl's arms and legs:

Arms: The arms consist of two ovals, each of which is just over half as long as the body. Her hands are shaped like upside-down teardrops.

Legs: Her legs consist of oval shapes. The upper leg is nearly as long as her body, while the lower leg is shorter and thinner. Her feet are drawn slightly turned outward, so use triangles.

D **Face:** The teenage girl's face is turned slightly away from us, so draw a curved faint line down her face, slightly offset to your right. This line represents the center of her face. Her features should be almost symmetrical—this means that whatever you draw on one side of her face, you should repeat on the other. Her eyes sit around halfway up her face.

5 G

6 H

Arms: To get the full shape of her arms, join the two ovals with a flowing outline. Next, her hands have a thumb in the center of each "teardrop."

E

Body: Girls have a curvier figure than boys, particularly older girls and women. Start to define the shape of her chest and waist—she has an "hourglass" figure.

Feet: Give her feet rounded toes with a flat base. These are going to be her sneakers.

Face: Start putting some detail on her face—the pupils in her eyes, some mid-length straight hair, and her ears.

Hands: Give the girl's hands more definition by drawing separate fingers, tucked in by her side.

Clothes: The tight tee shirt that the girl is wearing follows the contours of her body. Her biking shorts are also smooth, and they come to just above her knees. Give her shoes detail like the laces and soles. Don't forget to give her some socks!

F

Clothes: Now put the finishing touches to her clothes. Her tee shirt has a triangular logo on it, and she is wearing big earrings and a necklace. Give your girl a watch and some stripes running down the sides of her shorts. Lastly, make her socks really wrinkled.

Hands: Add some final definition to the fingers, such as long fingernails.

Body: Draw marks where her knees show, and add creases where her elbows bend.

G Draw over your teenage girl using a black pen and then erase the pencil lines. Now she's ready to color in!

H Because this girl is so sporty, she is wearing brightly colored clothing. Her top is lime green, and her shorts have bright red stripes running down them. You may, of course, use whatever colors you want —so experiment as much as you like!

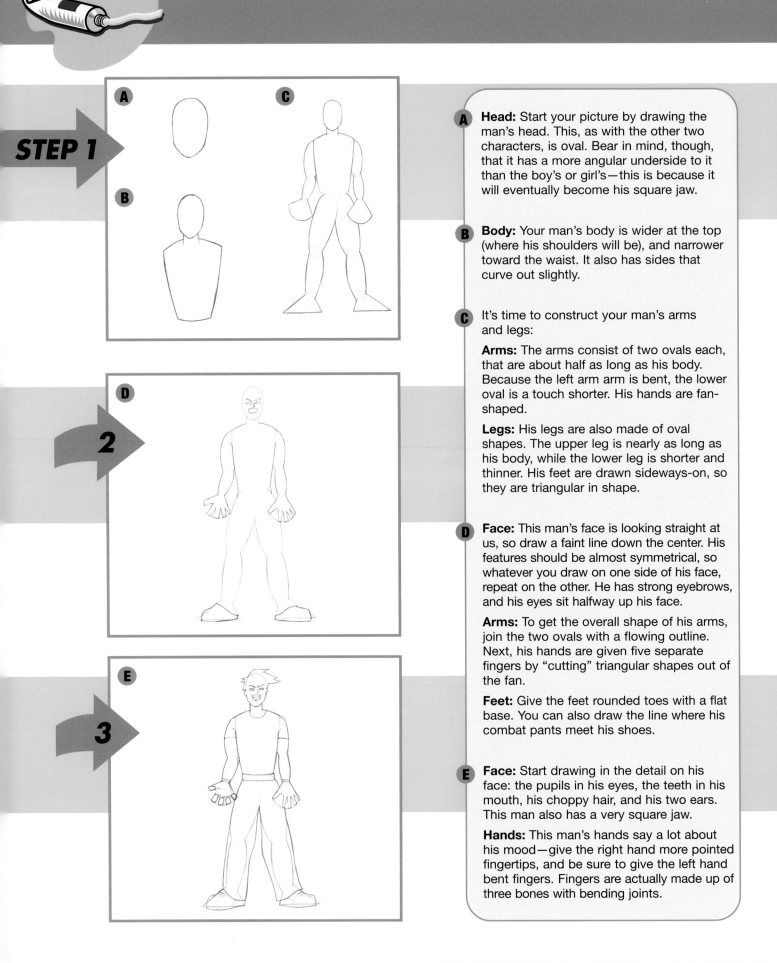

A **Head:** Start your picture by drawing the man's head. This, as with the other two characters, is oval. Bear in mind, though, that it has a more angular underside to it than the boy's or girl's—this is because it will eventually become his square jaw.

B **Body:** Your man's body is wider at the top (where his shoulders will be), and narrower toward the waist. It also has sides that curve out slightly.

C It's time to construct your man's arms and legs:

Arms: The arms consist of two ovals each, that are about half as long as his body. Because the left arm arm is bent, the lower oval is a touch shorter. His hands are fan-shaped.

Legs: His legs are also made of oval shapes. The upper leg is nearly as long as his body, while the lower leg is shorter and thinner. His feet are drawn sideways-on, so they are triangular in shape.

D **Face:** This man's face is looking straight at us, so draw a faint line down the center. His features should be almost symmetrical, so whatever you draw on one side of his face, repeat on the other. He has strong eyebrows, and his eyes sit halfway up his face.

Arms: To get the overall shape of his arms, join the two ovals with a flowing outline. Next, his hands are given five separate fingers by "cutting" triangular shapes out of the fan.

Feet: Give the feet rounded toes with a flat base. You can also draw the line where his combat pants meet his shoes.

E **Face:** Start drawing in the detail on his face: the pupils in his eyes, the teeth in his mouth, his choppy hair, and his two ears. This man also has a very square jaw.

Hands: This man's hands say a lot about his mood—give the right hand more pointed fingertips, and be sure to give the left hand bent fingers. Fingers are actually made up of three bones with bending joints.

4

F

In this picture, we can only see the end bone on each finger as it is bent inward toward the palm of his hand.

Clothes: This man is wearing a tight tee shirt and baggy combat pants. The shirt simply follows the outline of his body and arms. The pants, however, are loose-fitting and hang off of his waist, draping down over his legs. Give him a watch on one wrist and a belt around his waist.

F **Clothes:** The tight tee shirt shows the man's "six-pack"(his stomach muscles), and also features a large lightning bolt emblem on it. He has creased pants that wrinkle and gather on his shoes. Now give the shoes soles and laces.

Hands: Add some creases to the skin of the man's hands where they bend, and give him some fingernails.

Body: Add creases where his elbows bend, before drawing in his arm muscles and his collar bone, which sticks out through his tee shirt slightly.

G Once you're happy with the look of your man, you can draw over him using a black pen. Remember only to draw over the lines you want to keep, and then erase all the pencil lines. Your man will then be ready to color in.

→

5

G

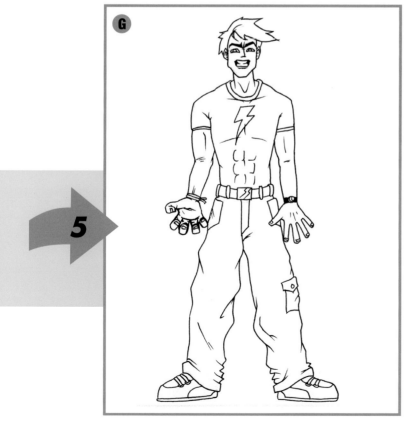

6

H Think about different color combinations before coloring your man in—look for shades that will go well together. In this picture, the man is wearing khaki combat pants and a dark blue tee shirt on which there is a yellow lightning bolt.

"Work hard, play hard." It is a great mantra to live by and hopefully, when you're not hard at work, you've got some sort of hobby—but if you're reading this, one of your hobbies must be drawing! Chances are though that you also have an interest in a sport, whether it be football, baseball, or skateboarding.

While sports are great to play or simply watch, it can also be a lot of fun drawing sporting characters. This section of the book is dedicated to helping you draw various sportsmen and women. It covers mainstream sports like football, basketball, and Formula 1 racing, but also deals with extreme sports such as surfing, snowboarding and skateboarding.

Maybe you want to draw your favorite sports hero or perhaps just a regular girl or guy enjoying their pastime. Either way, it'll be worth calling time on your busy day to check this out. So be on the ball, ride your creative wave, and bring these characters to life!

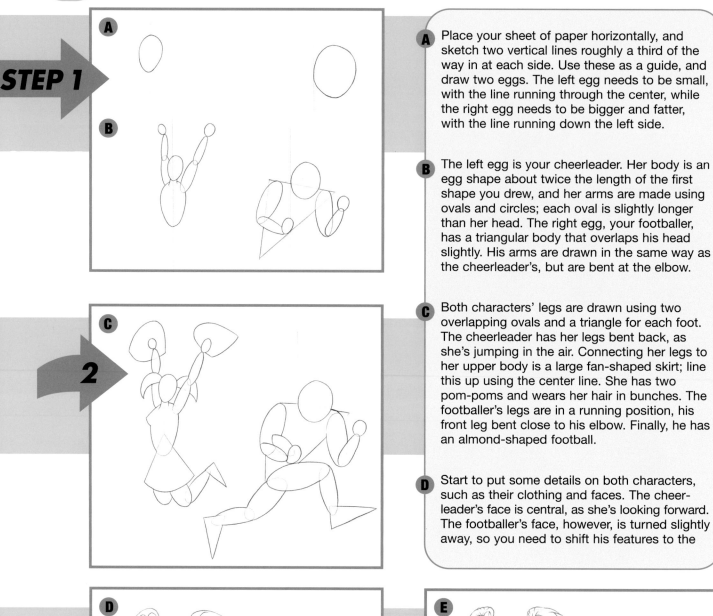

STEP 1

A Place your sheet of paper horizontally, and sketch two vertical lines roughly a third of the way in at each side. Use these as a guide, and draw two eggs. The left egg needs to be small, with the line running through the center, while the right egg needs to be bigger and fatter, with the line running down the left side.

B The left egg is your cheerleader. Her body is an egg shape about twice the length of the first shape you drew, and her arms are made using ovals and circles; each oval is slightly longer than her head. The right egg, your footballer, has a triangular body that overlaps his head slightly. His arms are drawn in the same way as the cheerleader's, but are bent at the elbow.

2

C Both characters' legs are drawn using two overlapping ovals and a triangle for each foot. The cheerleader has her legs bent back, as she's jumping in the air. Connecting her legs to her upper body is a large fan-shaped skirt; line this up using the center line. She has two pom-poms and wears her hair in bunches. The footballer's legs are in a running position, his front leg bent close to his elbow. Finally, he has an almond-shaped football.

D Start to put some details on both characters, such as their clothing and faces. The cheer-leader's face is central, as she's looking forward. The footballer's face, however, is turned slightly away, so you need to shift his features to the

3

4

5

F

E Your footballer's duds need to look authentic, so give his shirt a number on the front and sleeve, and you can also draw one on his helmet. Draw the stitching on the football, and give his boots a row of studs to help him grip the field. Give your cheerleader's pom-poms a fluffy look by drawing a spiky edge to them; her hair has a similar look. On both characters, draw pupils in the eyes and don't forget their teeth. These can be drawn with a single line through the center of the mouth.

F Before adding any color to your footballer and cheerleader, trace over your pencil version in black pen and erase the pencil lines. This prevents any smudging of the outline when you color them in.

right a little. His face is sketched lower down in your egg shape—the rest is his helmet. Round off both characters' feet to form their shoes and sketch the shape of their outfits. It's time to start drawing the final detail.

G Color your characters in your favorite team colors. The two characters here are wearing different colors, because the cheerleader is cheering for the rival team. That is making the footballer pretty mad!

6

G

STEP 1

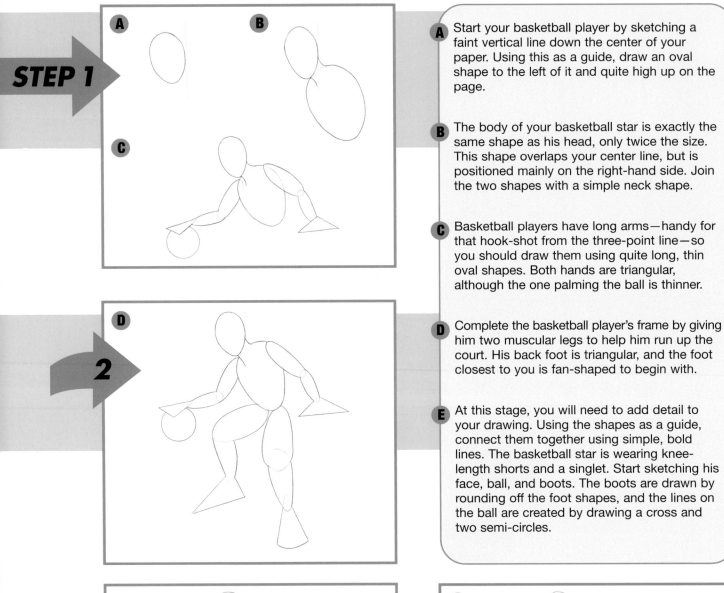

A Start your basketball player by sketching a faint vertical line down the center of your paper. Using this as a guide, draw an oval shape to the left of it and quite high up on the page.

B The body of your basketball star is exactly the same shape as his head, only twice the size. This shape overlaps your center line, but is positioned mainly on the right-hand side. Join the two shapes with a simple neck shape.

C Basketball players have long arms—handy for that hook-shot from the three-point line—so you should draw them using quite long, thin oval shapes. Both hands are triangular, although the one palming the ball is thinner.

2

D Complete the basketball player's frame by giving him two muscular legs to help him run up the court. His back foot is triangular, and the foot closest to you is fan-shaped to begin with.

E At this stage, you will need to add detail to your drawing. Using the shapes as a guide, connect them together using simple, bold lines. The basketball star is wearing knee-length shorts and a singlet. Start sketching his face, ball, and boots. The boots are drawn by rounding off the foot shapes, and the lines on the ball are created by drawing a cross and two semi-circles.

3

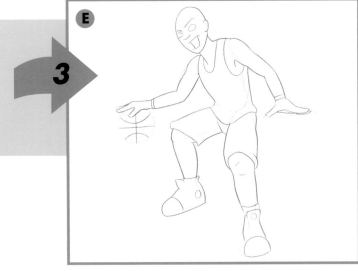

4

G

5

F Now it's time to finalize the detailing, specifically the designs on the basketball star's clothing and his facial features. Firstly, the face. He has a bald head, raised eyebrows, and almond-shaped eyes. The singlet has a large number on it and piping around the edges. The shorts have a stripe running down the length of the fabric. Finally, the laces on his sneakers are tied in a bow, and the sneakers have a separate rubber toecap.

G Now trace over all the lines you have drawn so far using a black pen. Then erase any pencil markings that are left. Your basketball star is now prepped and ready for coloring.

H

6

H Coloring this guy is easy. Just sit back and think of your favorite team and your favorite player. What are the team colors? If you don't have a favorite team, look around and see what colors are used often, or you could always just use the same colors as featured here.

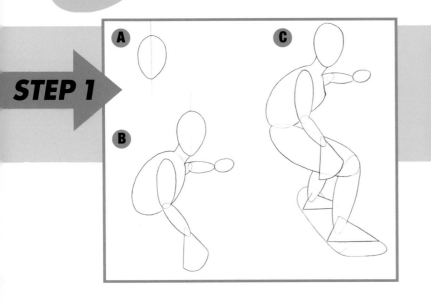

STEP 1

A Your skateboarder begins life as an egg shape with a vertical line running through the center. This egg is going to be her head, so it needs to be quite small and high up on the paper.

B The body of your skateboarding girl is also an oval shape, only it's about twice the size of her head—don't worry, you don't have to be exact! Her body is drawn to the left of your center line, diagonal to her head. Next, the left arm is drawn in front of the body, and consists of two long, thin ovals and a fan shape that is going to be her hand. Her other arm is partially hidden behind her body, so just draw the lower part of this limb.

C Now your skateboarder needs some legs to help her get around. The legs are created in a similar way to the arms, but with an added triangle at the base for the feet. As with the arms, one leg is prominent and the other is half-hidden. Finally, the board she's cruising on follows the line of her feet, and is slightly wider at the front to give a sense of depth.

D Draw your skater's outline using the shapes as a guide. Connect the shapes, remembering which ones are supposed to overlap and which ones aren't. Start sketching a face for your skateboarder—give her a huge smile and have her hair flowing behind her in the wind, which adds to the feeling of motion. Draw the individual fingers on the left hand using the

2

3

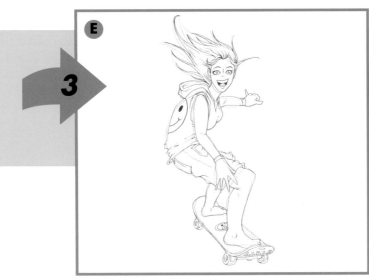

4

5

fan shape as a guide. She's wearing a hooded top and cut-offs. The skateboard's wheels are oval-shaped.

E Your skateboarder should be looking almost finished by now. To make her clothes look more realistic, draw creases where the wind is blowing the fabric, and where her body is hunched over. Her skateboard and top need some graphics. Remember, you can do whatever you want with the graphic—maybe put on the names of bands you're into or draw on some of your favorite cartoon characters.

F Once you're happy with the finished pencil sketch, you can draw over the pencil lines with a black pen, and erase any lines that you don't need.

G Color in your skateboarding girl using paints, colored pencils, felt-tip pens, or pastels. Using bright, strong tones really lifts your design up off of the page and adds to the positive atmosphere.

STEP 1

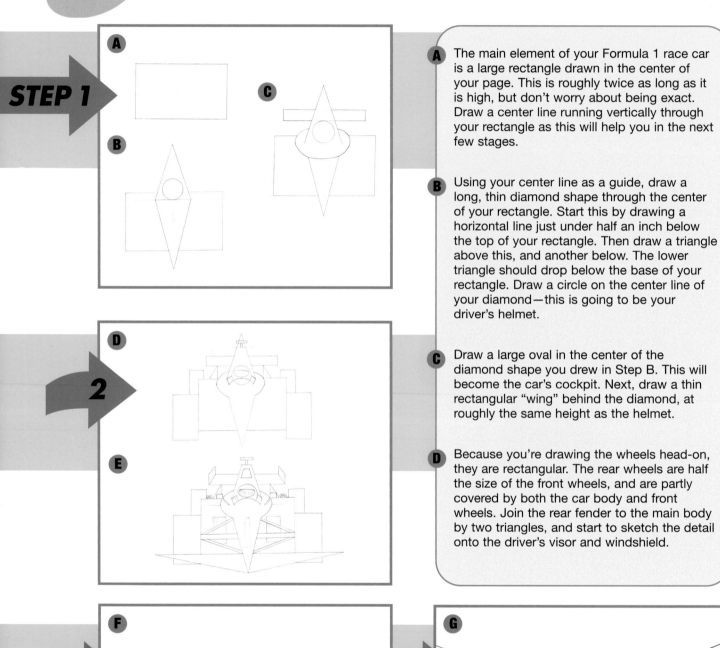

2

3

4

A The main element of your Formula 1 race car is a large rectangle drawn in the center of your page. This is roughly twice as long as it is high, but don't worry about being exact. Draw a center line running vertically through your rectangle as this will help you in the next few stages.

B Using your center line as a guide, draw a long, thin diamond shape through the center of your rectangle. Start this by drawing a horizontal line just under half an inch below the top of your rectangle. Then draw a triangle above this, and another below. The lower triangle should drop below the base of your rectangle. Draw a circle on the center line of your diamond—this is going to be your driver's helmet.

C Draw a large oval in the center of the diamond shape you drew in Step B. This will become the car's cockpit. Next, draw a thin rectangular "wing" behind the diamond, at roughly the same height as the helmet.

D Because you're drawing the wheels head-on, they are rectangular. The rear wheels are half the size of the front wheels, and are partly covered by both the car body and front wheels. Join the rear fender to the main body by two triangles, and start to sketch the detail onto the driver's visor and windshield.

E Chop the top off of your diamond shape and draw a tee-bar on top. Draw a vent below this, and turn up the edges of the rear fender. Next, draw side-mirrors on either side of the cockpit and sketch in your driver's face behind the visor. Finally, we move on to the front section of your car. The axles that connect each wheel to the chassis form a diamond shape. The front spoiler is a large, flat triangle, and the front vents are dark rectangles, hidden behind the axles.

F Round off those sharp edges—a F1 race car needs to be aerodynamic. The wheels are given a shine to make it look as if the track is wet,

5

and the car is covered in decals—a huge "No. 1" on the hood, with a smiley face and the words "Formula 1" across the rear fender.

G Draw over your F1 race car with a drawing pen, wait a few minutes for the ink to dry, and then erase any remaining pencil lines.

H The final stage of the picture involves adding the color. Use bright colors, as these will make your race car leap off the page—primary colors are great!

I Adding speed lines or drawing a close-up section of the cockpit will add dramatic impact to your race car. When only the driver and cockpit are

J showing, this shifts attention to the racer's expression of determination. In this kind of picture, only a suggestion of the car is needed.

6

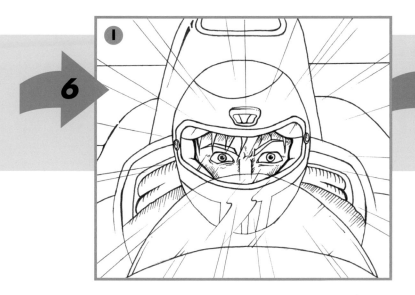

7

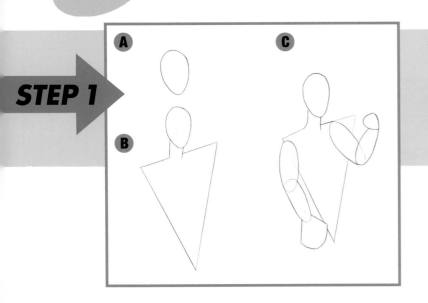

A Draw a faint vertical line down the center of your page. This is going to be helpful when placing the shapes that make up your surfer. Next draw an oval shape on the line, quite high up on the page.

B Your surfer's body is a large triangle shape, slanting over to the right so that the "shoulder" line lifts on the right-hand side. This is joined to the head by a simple two-line neck shape.

C It's time to give your surfer some arms. Draw two long ovals for each arm. The left arm is slightly bent, with a fan-shaped hand. His other arm is going to hold his surfboard, so it is bent at a sharper angle, with a semicircular hand ready to grab the rail.

2

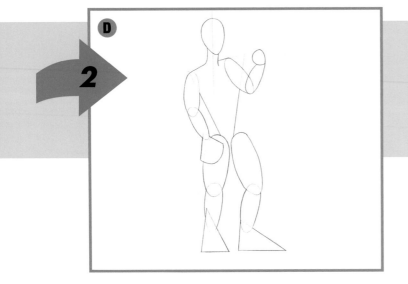

D The legs of your surfer are constructed in the same way as the arms—in three connecting shapes. These ovals should be about 1.5 times the length of those used for his arms, and a little wider too. His feet are triangular and the right leg should be slightly bent. The other leg is straight and lines up with the center line. This is his "weight-bearing" leg.

E Begin sketching in some simple detail, such as his wavy hair, his sweater, and his shorts. Use the arm and leg shapes as a template for drawing the outline of his clothes. Round off his triangular feet to form his shoes and draw where they meet his legs. Next, draw his

3

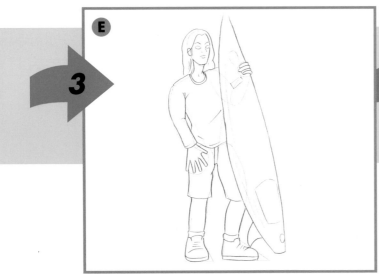

4

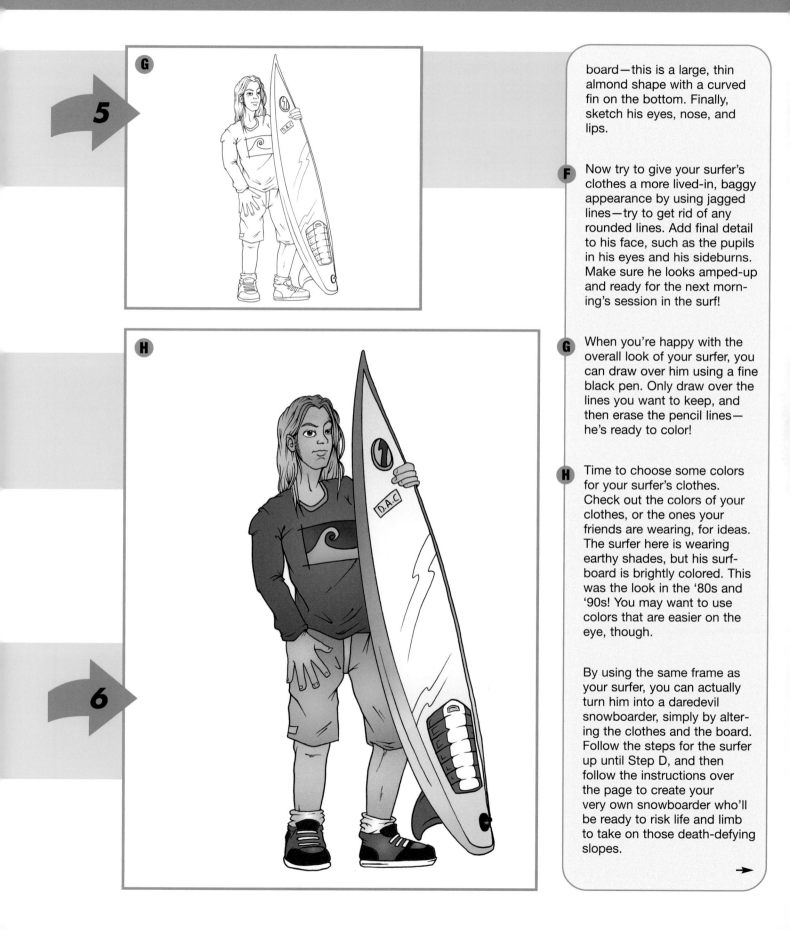

5

G

H

6

board—this is a large, thin almond shape with a curved fin on the bottom. Finally, sketch his eyes, nose, and lips.

F Now try to give your surfer's clothes a more lived-in, baggy appearance by using jagged lines—try to get rid of any rounded lines. Add final detail to his face, such as the pupils in his eyes and his sideburns. Make sure he looks amped-up and ready for the next morning's session in the surf!

G When you're happy with the overall look of your surfer, you can draw over him using a fine black pen. Only draw over the lines you want to keep, and then erase the pencil lines—he's ready to color!

H Time to choose some colors for your surfer's clothes. Check out the colors of your clothes, or the ones your friends are wearing, for ideas. The surfer here is wearing earthy shades, but his surfboard is brightly colored. This was the look in the '80s and '90s! You may want to use colors that are easier on the eye, though.

By using the same frame as your surfer, you can actually turn him into a daredevil snowboarder, simply by altering the clothes and the board. Follow the steps for the surfer up until Step D, and then follow the instructions over the page to create your very own snowboarder who'll be ready to risk life and limb to take on those death-defying slopes.

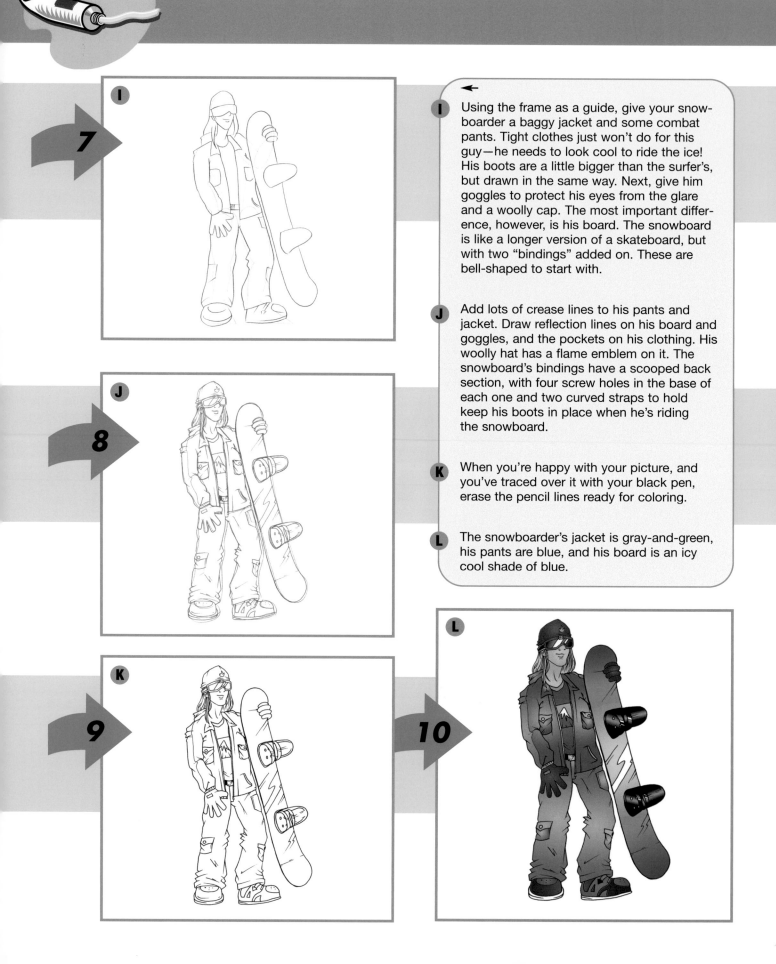

7 **I** Using the frame as a guide, give your snowboarder a baggy jacket and some combat pants. Tight clothes just won't do for this guy—he needs to look cool to ride the ice! His boots are a little bigger than the surfer's, but drawn in the same way. Next, give him goggles to protect his eyes from the glare and a woolly cap. The most important difference, however, is his board. The snowboard is like a longer version of a skateboard, but with two "bindings" added on. These are bell-shaped to start with.

8 **J** Add lots of crease lines to his pants and jacket. Draw reflection lines on his board and goggles, and the pockets on his clothing. His woolly hat has a flame emblem on it. The snowboard's bindings have a scooped back section, with four screw holes in the base of each one and two curved straps to hold keep his boots in place when he's riding the snowboard.

9 **K** When you're happy with your picture, and you've traced over it with your black pen, erase the pencil lines ready for coloring.

10 **L** The snowboarder's jacket is gray-and-green, his pants are blue, and his board is an icy cool shade of blue.

MANGA

Manga is a style of drawing that has become extremely popular throughout the world. It originated in Japan. The word "manga" means "comic art" in Japanese.

The manga style is very distinctive. Most of the female characters and younger characters are drawn with wide, glassy eyes and tiny noses. The men have slightly thinner features, and both men and women are often drawn with wild, spiky hair.

In this chapter, we're going to draw a manga team based on the sort of characters that you will find in most manga comics. Firstly, there is the hero, a kung-fu expert who is very confident and has real fighting spirit. Alongside him are his sidekicks, a female spy whose cunning gets her out of trouble, a robot (or "mecha") who is strong and intelligent, and a giant brown bear who is both loyal and hugely powerful.

After experimenting with the characters featured here, you may want to try designing your own manga characters. Those on the next few pages will give you some inspiration and you can add your own twist by altering the costumes or facial characteristics.

Remember, the key is to have fun and let your imagination run wild on the page. Anything is possible in a drawing, it's up to you to bring your ideas to life!

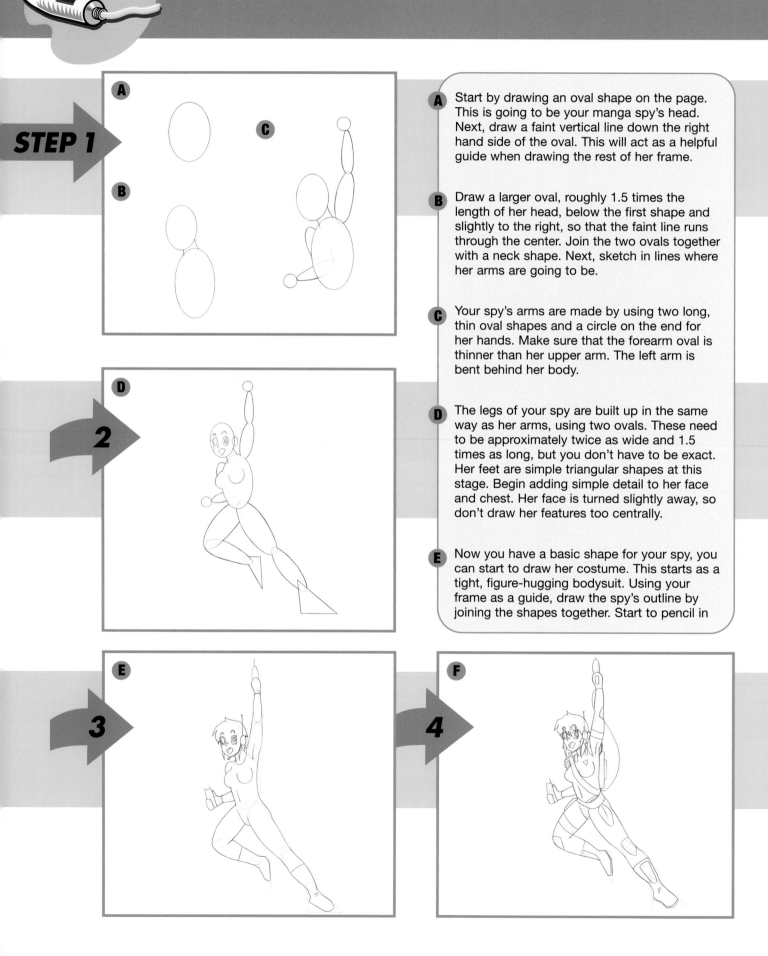

STEP 1

A Start by drawing an oval shape on the page. This is going to be your manga spy's head. Next, draw a faint vertical line down the right hand side of the oval. This will act as a helpful guide when drawing the rest of her frame.

B Draw a larger oval, roughly 1.5 times the length of her head, below the first shape and slightly to the right, so that the faint line runs through the center. Join the two ovals together with a neck shape. Next, sketch in lines where her arms are going to be.

C Your spy's arms are made by using two long, thin oval shapes and a circle on the end for her hands. Make sure that the forearm oval is thinner than her upper arm. The left arm is bent behind her body.

D The legs of your spy are built up in the same way as her arms, using two ovals. These need to be approximately twice as wide and 1.5 times as long, but you don't have to be exact. Her feet are simple triangular shapes at this stage. Begin adding simple detail to her face and chest. Her face is turned slightly away, so don't draw her features too centrally.

E Now you have a basic shape for your spy, you can start to draw her costume. This starts as a tight, figure-hugging bodysuit. Using your frame as a guide, draw the spy's outline by joining the shapes together. Start to pencil in

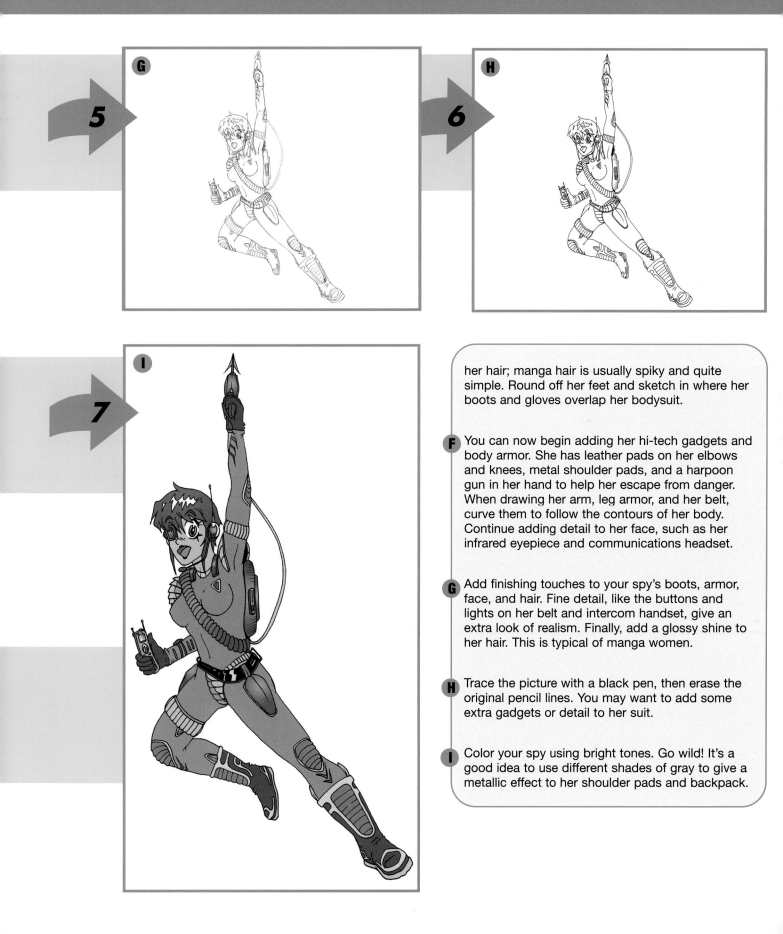

5

G

6

H

7

I

her hair; manga hair is usually spiky and quite simple. Round off her feet and sketch in where her boots and gloves overlap her bodysuit.

F You can now begin adding her hi-tech gadgets and body armor. She has leather pads on her elbows and knees, metal shoulder pads, and a harpoon gun in her hand to help her escape from danger. When drawing her arm, leg armor, and her belt, curve them to follow the contours of her body. Continue adding detail to her face, such as her infrared eyepiece and communications headset.

G Add finishing touches to your spy's boots, armor, face, and hair. Fine detail, like the buttons and lights on her belt and intercom handset, give an extra look of realism. Finally, add a glossy shine to her hair. This is typical of manga women.

H Trace the picture with a black pen, then erase the original pencil lines. You may want to add some extra gadgets or detail to her suit.

I Color your spy using bright tones. Go wild! It's a good idea to use different shades of gray to give a metallic effect to her shoulder pads and backpack.

STEP 1

2

3

4

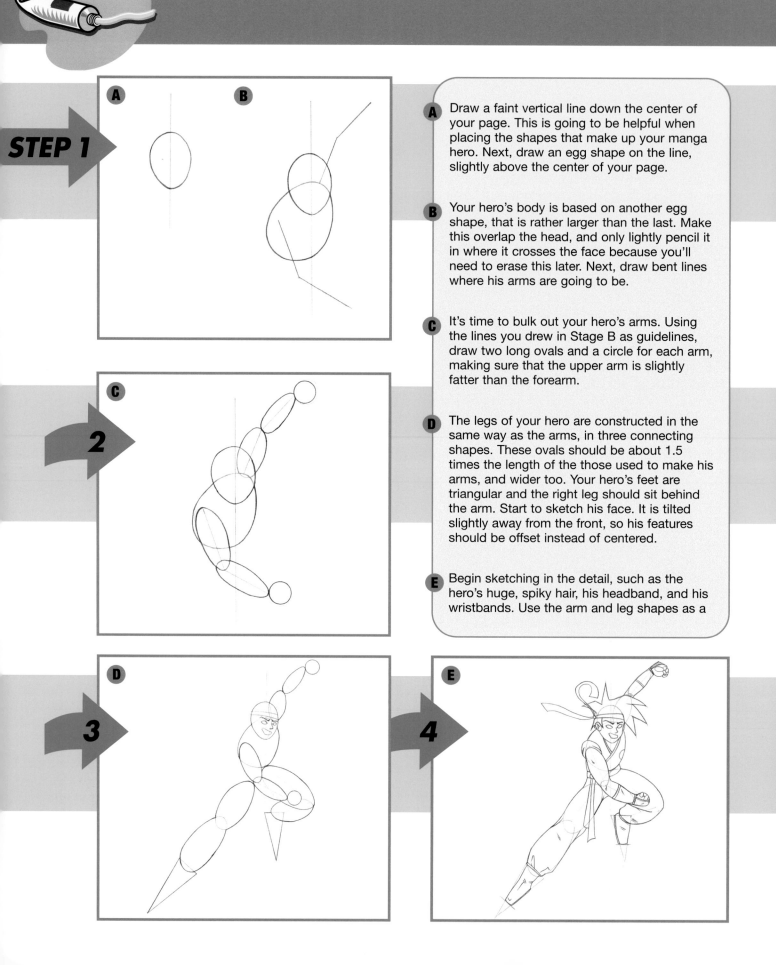

A Draw a faint vertical line down the center of your page. This is going to be helpful when placing the shapes that make up your manga hero. Next, draw an egg shape on the line, slightly above the center of your page.

B Your hero's body is based on another egg shape, that is rather larger than the last. Make this overlap the head, and only lightly pencil it in where it crosses the face because you'll need to erase this later. Next, draw bent lines where his arms are going to be.

C It's time to bulk out your hero's arms. Using the lines you drew in Stage B as guidelines, draw two long ovals and a circle for each arm, making sure that the upper arm is slightly fatter than the forearm.

D The legs of your hero are constructed in the same way as the arms, in three connecting shapes. These ovals should be about 1.5 times the length of the those used to make his arms, and wider too. Your hero's feet are triangular and the right leg should sit behind the arm. Start to sketch his face. It is tilted slightly away from the front, so his features should be offset instead of centered.

E Begin sketching in the detail, such as the hero's huge, spiky hair, his headband, and his wristbands. Use the arm and leg shapes as a

5

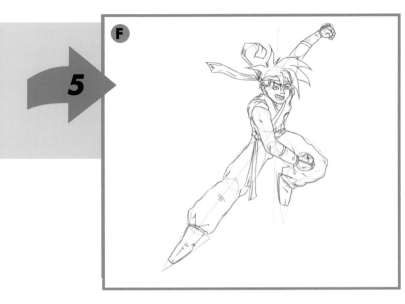

F

template for drawing the outline of his costume. Round off his triangular feet to form his boots and draw the lines where they meet his pants.

F Now, give your hero's costume a crisp but baggy appearance by using jagged lines. Try to get rid of any rounded lines on his suit. Add final detail to his face, such as the pupils in his eyes and his teeth. Then draw over him using a fine black pen. Erase the pencil lines, and he's ready for coloring.

G You can use any colors you like for his clothing, the ones shown here are just a suggestion. You can photocopy your drawing and experiment with different colors on the copies until you're satisfied.

6

G

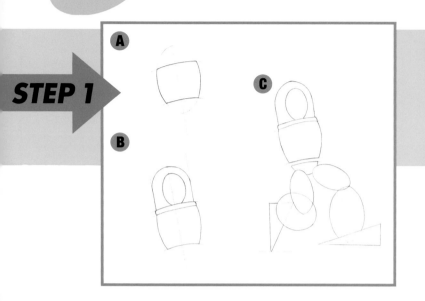

A Begin by sketching a large oval shape in the center of your page, placed at a slight angle. Draw a straight line through the center of this and trim the oval down to a barrel shape. This is going to be the main body of his spacesuit.

B Draw a dome shape on top of the body, with a rim along the base of it joining it to the spacesuit body. A compass or circular template may help when drawing the dome. Next, draw an oval shape inside the dome; this will be your astronaut's head.

C Your astronaut's legs are constructed using simple shapes. His feet are triangular, and the upper and lower parts of the leg are both oval-shaped. As the left leg is tucked back whilst running, make sure the shapes overlap each other. This will give depth to the picture and make it appear that he is striding forward.

2

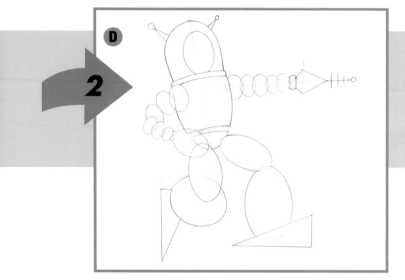

D The arms of the spacesuit are drawn using lots of overlapping ovals. Add a diamond-shaped laser on the right arm and a claw on the left arm. You can also put two antennae on his helmet, so he can pick up any transmissions from ground control.

E Round off your astronaut's triangular feet and begin putting detail onto the different sections of his legs, remembering which parts overlap each other. Start to sketch his facial features and spiky hair. Remember, his head is turned,

3

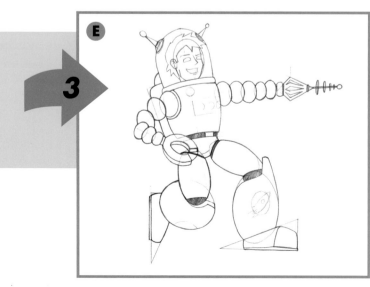

4

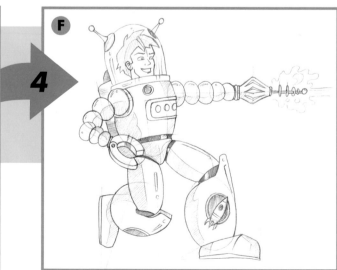

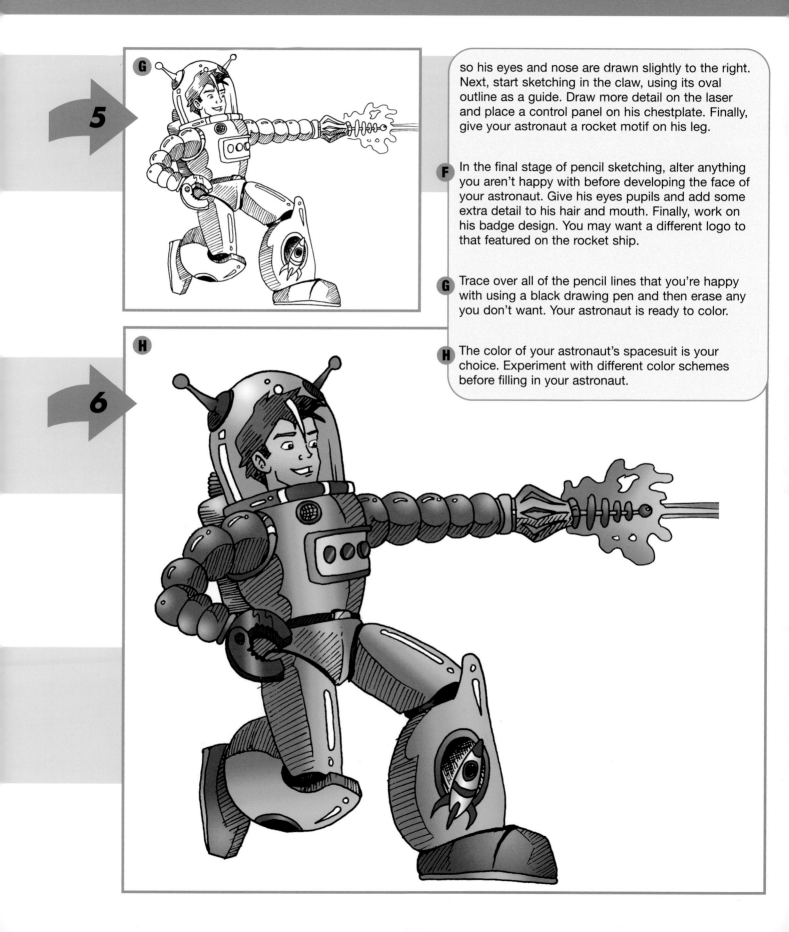

5

G

6

H

so his eyes and nose are drawn slightly to the right. Next, start sketching in the claw, using its oval outline as a guide. Draw more detail on the laser and place a control panel on his chestplate. Finally, give your astronaut a rocket motif on his leg.

F In the final stage of pencil sketching, alter anything you aren't happy with before developing the face of your astronaut. Give his eyes pupils and add some extra detail to his hair and mouth. Finally, work on his badge design. You may want a different logo to that featured on the rocket ship.

G Trace over all of the pencil lines that you're happy with using a black drawing pen and then erase any you don't want. Your astronaut is ready to color.

H The color of your astronaut's spacesuit is your choice. Experiment with different color schemes before filling in your astronaut.

STEP 1

A Start your drawing with a simple egg shape, with the pointed end facing downward. Remember that most human heads can be started in this way.

B Now, draw a large triangle beneath the head, joined by a "neck" consisting of two curved lines. Attach two arms to the triangular body. One arm is bent backward, while the other is thrusting forward. The arms are created using two ovals with a circle on the end of each, that are going to be her hands.

C Miss Velocity's body is completed by giving her two striding legs. One leg is out in front, bent at the knee. Remember to draw her upper leg wider than her lower leg, just like yours. Her other leg is stretched out behind her, so it must be drawn smaller and thinner to give the appearance of perspective. Finally, she needs triangular feet and curved lines to represent her chest and the curve of her back.

2

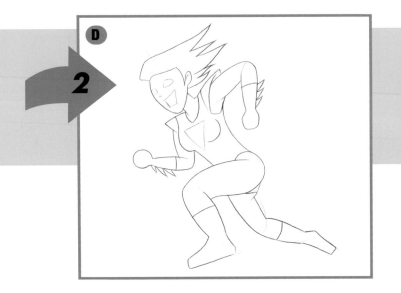

D This is where you begin working on Miss Velocity's details. Using your frame as a guide, start to round off the sharp edges on her feet and shoulders. Begin adding her facial features and her long, flowing hair. Draw a triangle on her chest where her logo is going to be, and give her gloves a row of spines.

E Start cleaning up the lines of Miss Velocity's body, and give her face, hair, and costume more detail. Separate her hair into sections, and give her a mask to hide her identity. Final touches, such as the letter "V" on her gloves,

3

4

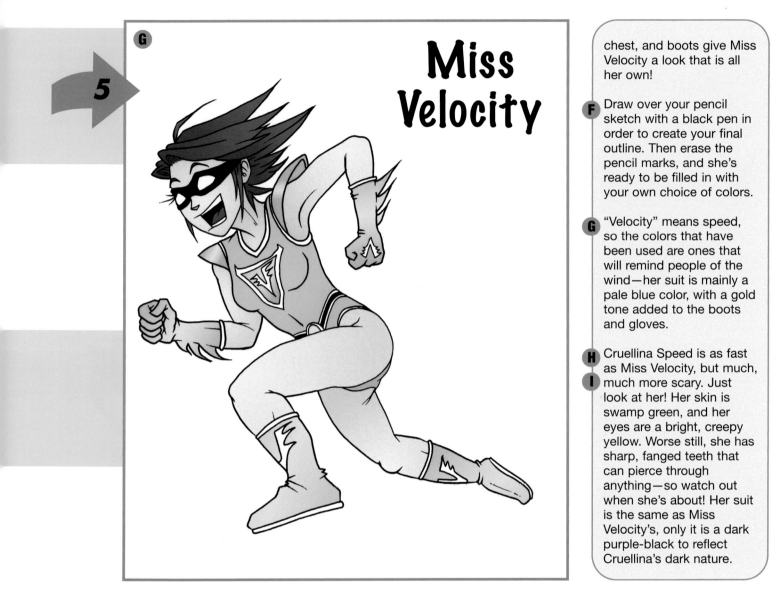

Miss Velocity

chest, and boots give Miss Velocity a look that is all her own!

F Draw over your pencil sketch with a black pen in order to create your final outline. Then erase the pencil marks, and she's ready to be filled in with your own choice of colors.

G "Velocity" means speed, so the colors that have been used are ones that will remind people of the wind—her suit is mainly a pale blue color, with a gold tone added to the boots and gloves.

H Cruellina Speed is as fast
I as Miss Velocity, but much, much more scary. Just look at her! Her skin is swamp green, and her eyes are a bright, creepy yellow. Worse still, she has sharp, fanged teeth that can pierce through anything—so watch out when she's about! Her suit is the same as Miss Velocity's, only it is a dark purple-black to reflect Cruellina's dark nature.

The main thing to remember is to have fun, and lots of it! Drawing different characters and scenes is really exciting, and all you need to begin with is a pencil and a sheet of paper.